CONVERSATIONS WITH MY SON

The Lion and His Cub

By:

OMEGA KAYNE

©™Omega Kayne Media 2015

Omega Kayne Media

All rights reserved. Except for use in any review, the reproduction or utilization of this work in whole or in part in any form by any electronic, mechanical, or any other means, not known or hereafter invented, including xerography, photocopying, and recording, or in any information storage or retrieval system, is forbidden without written permission of the publisher, Omega Kayne Media and the author Omega Kayne.

Copyright © 2015 by Omega Kayne

ISBN -13:- 978-0-9891851-7-2

ISBN-10: - 0-9891851-7-6

Manufactured in the United States

First Edition

Dedication

TO MY PRINCE

You are the son I always wanted. You bring so much happiness to my life and you make me and your mother so very proud. You have taught me so many things about myself that I never knew and have made me a better person. Because of you, I have learned how to LOVE unconditionally. You melt my heart when you call me "DADDY." You brighten my SPIRIT when you run to me and give me hugs. You give me LIFE when I look at you and see who you are becoming. I LOVE YOU SON, with every ounce of breath that I have in me and I will always let you know this. We are one and the same and our blood is ROYAL. As I've said to you many times, I AM THE KING and you ARE THE PRINCE. You are destined for greatness because it is in you. I will be there as your FATHER, DAD, PROTECTOR, and FRIEND.

Our bond will never be broken as I know that my happiness resides where our hearts beat. When I look at you, I see me all over again and you continue to make me proud. I want you to continue to be respectful to all. LOVE your Mother and protect her always. Be kind to others and know that our MOST HIGH has his hands on you and he will never forsake you son. You are the BLESSING that I will never take for granted. Every sacrifice I make has NOTHING to do with me because it is all for YOU. You will be a KING someday my PRINCE and it will all make sense to you then. I hope that you enjoy this book as I share with the world how magnificent you are. Loving you whether I'm NEAR or FAR.

YOU make me PROUD!

JAH BLESS

Acknowledgements

To EVERYONE who has ever SUPPORTED ME in all of my ventures throughout the years. To those who allowed me to sleep on their floors and couches, RENT FREE I thank you. To those who let me borrow money when my times were hard without hesitation and you offered it because you knew my pride was going to be the death of me...THANK YOU.

To those who continue to pray for me, praise me, follow me, and share my gift with others...THANK YOU. Because of you, I can do what I LOVE. I appreciate all of you who have had a hand in my success.

Thank You to the QUEEN for being the vessel the MOST HIGH chose to give us a handsome Prince. You will always be the MOTHER of our SON and I will hold the highest regard toward you as we raise a KING in waiting. Blessings to you forever.

And to the MOST HIGH....MY JAH.

You have shown me who you are and I BELIEVE. THANK YOU for never giving up on me when I have constantly fallen short of your grace Father. I ask that you keep me in FAVOR and keep the SHINE on me. NONE of this would be happening if it wasn't for your MERCY.

CHAPTERS

1. I Prayed For You.................... 6

2. The Day You Arrived............. 13

3. The Bond We Share............... ..19

4. You Taught Me Unconditional Love 25

5. My Life Without You................33

6. From a King to A Prince………..39

7. Always My Baby Boy...............44

8. The Tears I've Cried.................49

9. My Prayers Are For You………..62

10. Love and Protect Your Mommy..................................68

Epilogue................................76

~CHAPTER ONE~

I PRAYED FOR YOU

You probably won't believe this son but there was once a time when I thought I didn't want a child. I look back at that time in my life and I laugh now because I have you. But I also prayed to GOD that if I ever were to become a father to give me a healthy, handsome boy. And being the GOD that He is, He BLESSED me and your mother with the MOST PRECIOUS GIFT that any parent could receive. I PRAYED FOR YOU. God answered me and I've been the happiest man on Earth ever since.

From day one, we connected and our heartbeats have been in synch ever since. It is amazing to me how much you mean to me and how much control you have over me. You have made me laugh. You have made me cry. You have made me proud and excited with every new milestone that you achieve.

I wouldn't change a thing about our relationship because it is pure and genuine. When you came into my life, it forever changed me and even when my road was rocky, you kept me going.

Do you know that to this day I spend hours looking at the hundreds of pictures that we have together? There are so many that I secretly snapped when you would crawl on my chest and fall asleep. I knew that these were moments to savor because in those quiet times the reality of having a son would hit and remind me that I was responsible for this little life and I LOVED IT! I would spend hours while you slept because I couldn't get any rest and I just watch you breathe and move around. You brought me peace Son and God knows I needed it.

Some of those pictures bring tears to my eyes because they remind me of the moments we created together when you were just a baby. You were an amazing baby and you rarely cried. In fact, you loved to laugh.

I'm so glad I grew up and changed my mind about wanting to be a parent. I didn't smile a lot until you came into my life and now I can't stop when I'm around you. I look at you today and I laugh hysterically because you are exactly like me. You have the artist spirit. You have a great personality and people love to be around you. Son, you are everything that a parent wishes for when they have children and I am so glad that I PRAYED FOR A SON LIKE YOU.

I want to thank you for brightening my days and giving me something to look forward to every day of my life. You have opened my mind to many possibilities in life upon which I want to build an empire for you.

You will be successful because I am drawing the blueprint that will guide you. You will be resourceful because I will be your example and lead the way. You will be remarkable because it's in your bloodline and you are favored. You will be a great man because I will lay the foundation for you. God will BLESS you because he is in the blessing business and he made me your father. I will never turn away from you Son and my love will remain unconditional. You are awesome and you make your dad very proud.

I could never imagine not having you in my life. It would tear me apart if I could not hear your voice or give you a hug.

EVERY SINGLE TIME you call me, "DADDY," you make me smile and you soften my heart. That was something that rarely happened in the past.

Before you were born I wasn't a sensitive man but I believe that God knew I needed to be. I also believe that he knew the only way to bring out the sensitivity in me was to give me someone that I would love more than myself…YOU my son.

You are too young to understand this now but as you grow older it will all make sense. You truly saved my life. Not only are you my son but you are my ANGEL. Thank You.

I LOVE YOU.

~CHAPTER TWO~

The Day You Arrived

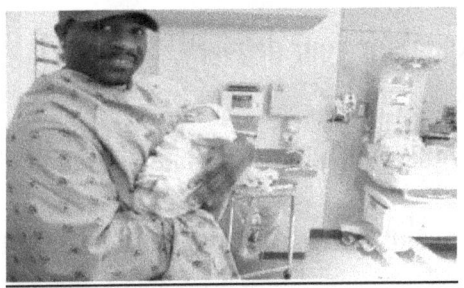

When your mother looked at me after her water broke, I knew that it was time. We already had her overnight bags packed and we were prepared to bring you into this world. Deep down inside I was afraid not because we were about to have you but because I knew that our lives would be changed forever! I was afraid that we didn't have any experience with taking care of a baby and now we'd gone from dress rehearsals to the real thing. In complete control, your dad made sure we had everything and drove your mother to the hospital for your delivery.

Son, your mom handled childbirth like a pro. Yes, she was in obvious pain because of her contractions but she remained strong. She surprised me because she didn't receive an epidural until the very last minute. She was determined to bring you into the world and as much as I tried to remain strong for her by consoling her and holding her hand, I still couldn't imagine the pain she was in. But, she showed me her resilience and strength as tears rolled down her face with each contraction, enduring the labor pains like a champion. All the while I was like a spectator watching and praying that all would be well and knowing that there was nothing that I could do but allow the process to happen. In those moments, I knew that her strength combined with mine would be passed on to you and you would be a little warrior.

We waited for hours for your arrival. I'm laughing now because as your mom was having contractions; the doctor remained calm, telling us that we still had a while before you'd be born.

This process was very new to me and your mom as first-time parents, so we relied on what the doctor told us. When the doctor turned away to prepare her instruments, she said, "He's not ready yet," but I saw differently. YOU WERE READY NOW!

I saw your little head about to enter the world and said to the doctor, "Isn't that his head? He's coming now!" From that point on, everything moved in fast forward mode and, before long, I heard the cries of my baby boy.

I don't know exactly what I was thinking in that moment. I was very excited but I was also nervous and scared. When I saw you for the first time I became overwhelmed with pride and thankful to God.

I asked for some scrubs to hold you after the attending nurses cleaned you up. Your mother still jokes about me asking for those scrubs because she thought I was concerned about messing up my shirt but honestly, none of that mattered because you were finally here and I had my son in my arms for the very first time.

I couldn't believe that I was holding MY child. I was finally meeting you after seeing you move in your mommy's belly for months. Finally, you were here, alive and kicking, in my arms. This still stands as one of the greatest moments of my life.

You can't see it in the picture, but I cried like a baby. I tried my best to keep everyone in the room from seeing this big, strong guy cry by quickly wiping the tears of joy that your birth had brought me from my eyes. I knew then that I would always LOVE and PROTECT YOU!

I LOVE YOU!

~CHAPTER THREE~

The Bond We Share

The first two years of your life it was just you and me every day while Mommy went back to work. I was so scared the first day she left me there to take care of you. I wish you could have seen my face as she walked out the door.

I was clueless about what I should do. I just knew that, somehow, I had to keep you fed and clean, plus make sure we both got sleep during the day and that was exactly what that first day was all about.

I was working actor but work had slowed down for me, so I was able to stay home with you. Although it saved us money to not put you in daycare, it still was a high-pressure situation for a macho guy with no prior experience caring for a baby.

I have to admit to you, Son, it was a very hard time for daddy because although I wanted to be home to take care of you. I also wanted to be out working doing what I loved so that I help provide for the family but it didn't work as planned. I truly had my share of "MAN moments," where my pride and ego would be constantly eating away at me. This is something you will deal with later in life, but no need to worry about that now. Just enjoy being a kid and let your parents shoulder the burdens for you.

After a few weeks, we worked out our routine. We'd wake up each morning. I'd feed and change you, if I needed too. Sometimes I would give you a warm bath or wipe down. You were a good baby, like I said before, and you really didn't cry much. After your feeding, we would play or I would take you for a scroll in the neighborhood and to the park then we would come back and we'd take our daily nap.

This was my favorite time of day because I was just as tired as you were and I looked forward to getting some sleep. During the night, Mommy would get up and tend to you when you would awaken, but sometimes Daddy would get up too because I knew she had to go to work the next morning. I was a very light sleeper so anytime you moved or cried, I would immediately awaken anyway. I was so protective over you, my prince.

As we took our daily naps, I tried to sleep but in those first months I was still going through my "paranoid papa" stage so you almost always slept next to me or on my chest. I have at least two hundred pictures of you in that position and I loved you being there, close to my heart. You got so used to sleeping in this position that as you got a little older, you would just crawl to me on the bed and lie across my chest at nap time.

This was truly our bonding time and I enjoyed every minute of it. Yes, I wanted to be the man of the house and provide you and mommy with all that you needed, but it just didn't work out like that. God wanted me home with you every day so that we could build our relationship.

It didn't make sense at first and I fought it because I was allowing my pride to get the best of me. But now that I look back at that time in our lives, I see that God knew what He was doing. He kept me unemployed for a reason. He knew that we would have a special bond and that someday I would write about it. Imagine that!

I LOVE YOU!

~CHAPTER FOUR~

You Taught Me Unconditional Love

The day you were born, I fell in LOVE with you. Nobody told me I had too, it just happened. There was this overwhelming feeling deep inside my soul that just connected me to you and I knew immediately that this connection was different. I knew you were a part of me and it was my duty, as your father, to be there for you.

I have never felt love like this before. I mean, I've said "I love you" many times in my life and although each time I said it I meant it, this love that I have for you is very different from anything I've ever felt before. Again, when I hear you call me "Daddy," it still melts me like butter.

You bring out feelings in me that I've always wanted to have with my father when I was your age, which is another reason why I love you so much. You are giving me something I've never had; A real father-son relationship. Hopefully, as you grow older, you'll come to know that I'm giving you everything that I wish I had gotten from my father.

Every son will seek a relationship with and approval from their father. And, someday, when you become a father you can refer to this book and say, "Now I see what my dad meant by this."

One thing I do know for sure, Son, is that I made a conscious choice to be a solid fixture in your life. I'm not going anywhere and I will never abandon you for any reason. I will be present; I will be vocal; and you will always know that you are important in my life no matter where I am or what I'm doing. I will raise you to be a strong, respectable, human being, even if that means scolding you sometimes.

Most of all, I will share moments and make memories with you so that you will have those stories to tell when you get older. Our relationship will mean more to you than just having a father who shows up on holidays and birthdays, or a father who just sends gifts. That may be OK for some; that may work for many but I never want that to be my relationship with you. I will always be a part of your life; not just because it's my responsibility, but because I want to be your hero, your protector, and your greatest example of manhood. I couldn't imagine my life without you Son and no matter the circumstances, I will always be your father and I will always be here for you.

Although we are not together as a full family, it does not change my love for you or commitment to you. Mommy and I are working as a team to raise you. I have been homeless just to be close to you. I have given my last dollars to make sure I did my part as your dad to help mommy clothe you and buy gifts for your birthdays and holidays as well as school supplies and uniforms. It was you who brought that kind of selflessness out of me. Jordan you taught me how to love through a storm.

I have so many stories that I want to tell you that will amaze you once you're old enough for us to sit down and talk.

I will always try to position myself well in order to help mommy do all the things that are necessary to raise you. Even if I don't have it at the time that she needs it, I will do my best to hurry and get it because you are also my responsibility. This help goes way beyond financial responsibilities, though.

I will be available to answer the questions that only a dad can answer. I will be there when she needs some time to breathe and take time out for herself. I will be there for protection and guidance, as well as discipline and praise. Your mom and I will do this together as a team.

THIS IS WHAT UNCONDITIONAL LOVE IS and this is what I have learned as your father. You taught me this. I LOVE YOU more than I love myself and no matter the circumstance, please know that I, your father, will work tirelessly to provide for you.

I NEEDED you in my life. Because of you my priorities and how I see the world have changed. You became first in my life when you were born and it was then that I began to make plans to build an empire for you...and I will not stop until I'm successful in doing so.

Know this, too, Son. Everyone will not understand your path in life, but if you feel a strong conviction in what you want to do for your happiness, do what is right for your spirit. No matter what, my love for you will remain **UNCONDITIONAL.**

I LOVE YOU!

~CHAPTER FIVE~

My Life without You

You not being in my life would be like me not being able to breathe. I would suffocate and die of a broken heart. When I think of not having you as my son, I break down and fall into silence because I can't imagine my life without you in it. When we are together everyone sees our deep connection. Your mother says you are just like me and I see it too.

It's amazing that you have taken on my character traits and personality. I sit back and just listen to you talk. I watch how you deal with others and how others are attracted to your personality. You are a little superstar and just to think, I've never pushed my interests on you. I've never said to you that I wanted you to be a football player or an actor but you seem to have the desire, the interest, and the talent to do both.

When you sing and dance and I can see where you get it from. Mommy can dance and daddy can too. I have a little bit of a singing voice or at least I think I do! But, mostly, I'm just enjoying watching you grow into a fine young man who has his own interests. You are your own person and I will respect your choices in life. You are your own person and whatever goals you set in life, I will be there to help you achieve them.

I couldn't imagine not being there for you, not giving you advice or pointers. I get a kick out of listening to you explain your games to and how you play them. I laugh at how, when I'm winning, you quickly restart the game so that you can try to beat me. I LOVE your competitive spirit.

I remember going to your karate class and seeing how much you were into it. You are very good and tough. You made me so proud and while you were sparring, I didn't have any concern about you getting hurt. I guess it's a "dad" thing, but I wanted you to experience this without me swooping in to save you, so I just sat back and cheered you on while keeping a watchful eye.

I also saw how having me there sometimes affected your performances. You wanted to be perfect but sometimes you messed up and were worried about disappointing me. I want you to know that it's OK not to be perfect.

You will mess up and fall short at times. I have failed many times, in many things. Although it may have hurt my feelings to mess up, I kept going and that's what I always want you to understand. Just because you may have failed doesn't mean that you are a failure. It also doesn't mean you should QUIT.

YOU ARE NOT A QUITTER. YOU ARE A CRUISE MAN, remember? We don't quit! We will be successful! We will take on challenges and we will win! Again these are lessons I learned on my own as a young boy and this is what I will instill in you. If you ever have any questions or any doubts, know that you can come to your father for answers and reassurances. There will never be anything that you cannot talk to me about. I will never judge you and I will never respond in anger if we have a difference of opinion either, I will respect who you are no matter your age.

I will respect your opinions. If you ever come across anyone who tries to change your mind about something you strongly believe in, Son, then that person doesn't have your best interest at heart. **THEY HAVE ONLY THEIR OWN.**

I could not imagine not being in your life to share these lessons with you.

I LOVE YOU!

~CHAPTER SIX~

From A King to a Prince

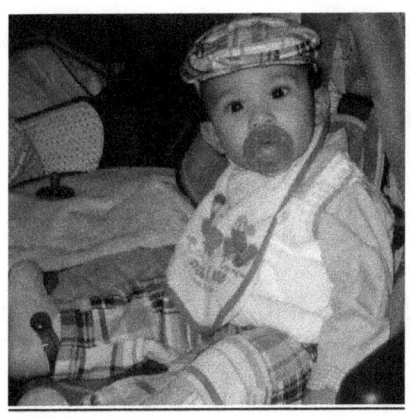

YOU ARE A PRINCE, and daddy is a King. You are royalty, Son. Your heritage comes from Kings and Queens. I want you know that you are more than what you will see in this harsh world.

The world will call you other names. Others will attempt to erase your history. They will fail to tell you truths about where you came from, so I will say to you now: Seek your own knowledge. It is ok to ask question about things that don't seem right no matter who is giving you the information.

Never just take someone's word and be OK with that, even if it's me. I will never be mad at you for seeking knowledge or challenging me. I do it all the time because I'm not a follower and you won't be either. I'm instilling in you leadership qualities. I'm teaching you that when you have something to say, it should make sense so that people will want to listen to you. I will teach you how to research even the most challenging questions because you shouldn't believe everything that is presented to you.

You will be the exception to the rule, my Prince. You will defy what society is attempting to portray you as. You are not a thug. You are a human being who has parents who care about you. You are a valuable being.

As my son I will hold you to the highest of standards. I will test you and challenge you because someday you, too, will be a King. I want to prepare you so that every move that you make will be dignified. I will teach you how to walk straight and stand strong.

Give firm handshakes and look a man in the eye when you talk to him. I will teach you that giving your word is more valuable than money for you will be remembered for what you say and do.

I'm going to teach you the value in respecting others, especially women. Never argue with or yell at a woman. **NEVER EVER** abuse any woman, no matter how angry one may make you. **WALK AWAY**, period.

You will say "please" and "thank you." You will be respectful to adults and address them as "Sir" or "Ma'am." You will not be known as a thug. You will not speak in broken English or walk around with your pants hanging low. You will behave like a gentleman at all times, according to the examples that I try to set for you. You want to be respected.

I don't drink alcohol and I don't do drugs of any kind. I would hope that you follow in my footprints when it comes to that. I want you to be someone that others look up too. I want you to be the person they seek advice from. I want you to be the man that society is trying to sweep underneath the rug as they try to pretend that men like us don't exist. YES WE DO. I AM one of those MEN and you will be too. You are a PRINCE and I am a KING.

I LOVE YOU!

~CHAPTER SEVEN~

<u>Always My Baby Boy</u>

As I write this book you are a vibrant and intelligent six year old. You are no longer a little boy and you have made it clear that you don't like to be called that. You are not a small baby, either. You are officially my big boy. But, guess what, son? You will ALWAYS be my baby boy no matter how old you are. But I accept that you're slowly becoming a young man.

On the other hand, your mother will always be in "mommy mode" and will want to treat you like her little baby because that's what mothers do. So, let her!

I will scream it to the world how proud you make me feel. I tell your mom all the time that we truly have been blessed with a remarkable child. You make us both feel so happy and fulfilled. I know that someday you will grow to be a fine young man.

You are growing more and more each day and we see you becoming a remarkable person. I believe all parents fear their children growing up and leaving because of the attachment that they have but I'm excited to see you grow up and how you handle what life has in store for you. I know that you will be fine, but be rest assured that mommy and daddy will be near to keep a watchful eye on you.

As I said before, I spend many late night hours looking at pictures of you, making collages and putting our names and dates on them because I want you to see them and know that you and I have always been a team. I want you to see that I cherished our moments together and immortalized them in frames and photo albums so that one day we can sit back and laugh at those memories.

There shouldn't be any doubt in your mind how I feel about you, Son. You are my world and my reason for living. My life's purpose now is to find ways to make your dealings with the world as seamless as possible.

I know that your mother and I won't be able to save you from every bad thing in the world, but we will certainly try to save you from the ugliest parts of it because we want to see you succeed and do better than we've done.

I'm still in awe that I have a son but I'm so blessed that God gave me you. You are an absolute joy and delight to have in my life and you truly brighten my day.

I remember making up a little song to sing to you when you were a baby. I sang that song to you every night. When you were about four years old, you started humming and trying to sing along. When you turned five, you were fully singing the song with me, soon making up your own version by replacing the words that I sang using your name with "Mommy" and "Daddy." Now that you are six years old, you still ask me to sing that song to you before you go to bed. So, you see, no matter how old you are, my prince, I will sing that song to you because you will always be my baby boy!

I LOVE YOU!

~CHAPTER EIGHT~

The Tears I've Cried

Where do I begin, my prince? I've never cried as much in my life as I have since you've come into my world. I was never sensitive. In fact, I was a bit stoic when I dealt with people.

But when you arrived, God put something in me that I clearly needed. I needed to know how to express my feelings. I needed to understand that it was OK for a man to cry and show emotion.

Do you remember when I said that you truly saved my life? Well, I'm going to tell you a couple of stories that I know you don't remember but when you get older and re-read this book, you can ask me about them.

There were more than a few times when I cried my heart out where it concerned you, but these few times really stuck in my mind. The first time I truly broke down and cried was when I left California to go and work in Atlanta. You were two years old and extremely attached to me.

I purposely chose to leave at night when you were asleep because I knew if I would have left while you were awake it would have been hard on the both of us. It was a very hard night for us for many reasons, but it was something that daddy had to do.

I kissed you on your forehead as you slept, then left. It didn't take long for my heart to begin hurting. My body became hot and nervousness overcame me.

I couldn't help what was about to happen in the next few minutes of my trip. I tried to hold it back but I just couldn't. I was leaving you so that I could go and work, but I didn't know when I would return or the next time I was going to see you.

I immediately started crying. I couldn't stop bawling because I had left you behind and you were the source of my happiness and joy. I must have cried, uncontrollably, for about a hundred miles.

I swear I hadn't felt that much pain in my life. Although I knew I needed to go, I still felt guilty for leaving you. Although I knew I would return, I still felt like you wouldn't understand why daddy had to go. You were still a baby and I knew you wouldn't understand at that age my reasons but I honestly felt like having that conversation with two-year-old as I thought it would help me make peace with my decision. I needed you to understand that I wasn't leaving your life or giving up on my responsibility to you, I was only trying to make it better.

Another thing that you may not know is that I allowed you, a two year old to determine a lot of decisions for me as well. There were times that I felt my heart drop out of my chest when I was away and I'd talk to you on the phone. I knew we were missing each other.

As you got older and began to talk and put words together in small sentences, I made it my business to always call you so that you would hear my voice or facetime you so that we could see each other's faces. I never wanted you to get use to me being gone.

But, one day we were talking on the phone and out of the blue, you said to me, "Daddy, I miss you. I want to see you!" Hearing you say those words to me hurt, and the only thing I could do at that moment was break down and cry.

It was December 22nd and I had very little money saved but after that conversation, my impulses took over. The very next morning I got on the road and drove over forty hours from Atlanta back to Los Angeles to surprise you for Christmas.

When I turned on our street I called mommy and told her that I was outside but not to tell you. She was also surprised that I was there, and when I walked in, your brown eyes just lit up and I fell in love with you all over again. If you look at the picture above, this was the morning that I drove in. My eyes were swollen from crying and I was dead tired from nonstop driving but none of that mattered when you jumped into my lap on Christmas morning hugging and kissing me.

YOU DO THAT TO ME. You have the power to stop me from doing what I NEED to do so that I can pay attention to you. NOBODY has ever had that much power over me. A big part of that is because I sincerely want to be a great father to you. I never want to disappoint you by lack of effort. You matter to me, first and foremost and I want to give you what I never had: A true and genuine, loving and involved father-son relationship.

    This last story that I will share with you is about when I flew back into town to see you. It would be a few days at a time and I always hated the departure. Your mom and I made a conscious effort to try and prepare you before I got there, telling you that daddy was going to leave on a certain day so that you could try and understand. You would always say that you understood, but when it was time for me to walk away, you would break down. I mean you would really break down and cry your little heart out. I couldn't take seeing you like that as I tried to hide my own tears, but the water wouldn't stop falling. As I walked away after kissing and hugging you nothing but pain would overcome me.

Minutes after I left, I'd call mommy to check on you and she'd tell me that you were still crying. Days later, mommy would say that you were still upset and you would be physically sick. Guilt would overcome over me again because I never wanted to make you feel that way.

You were still too young to comprehend life and adult responsibilities. All you wanted was to be with me. That's all that mattered to you.

This went on for a while until you got a little older and understood better that daddy would always return when he said he would.

I have always kept my word to you, and I will continue too. A father's word to his son should mean more than just words. Actions are reality for children and I learned how true that is when I was a boy because I never saw consistency in actions from my own father.

Many nights I've put myself in situations that were not safe so that I could be close to you.

When you get older I'll tell you about when I was homeless. I'll tell you about how I slept in my truck, hungry with very little money for food, because all of my money went to help take care of you. I'll tell you about the time that someone tried to break into my truck but didn't know that I was inside, sleeping, and how that led to my decision to do something different to make life better for US. I'll tell how high my blood pressure got and I had to go the emergency room to get immediate attention and the doctors told me that I could have easily died with pressure that high. I WAS UNDER STRESS and it caused my body to break down in ways that I never knew that it could.

I had to finally become comfortable in knowing that you were going to be all right without me around every day and for me to be OK with leaving again to make a better life. I had to understand that you were not going to feel like I abandoned you or failed you because I was not there to see you off to school every day. I had to feel comfortable in knowing that you knew that I was going to always be your father, no matter the physical distance between us.

I just cared about you, Son, and loved you so much that I was willing to put myself in harm's way so that I could see you and be around you, even when I'd lost everything else that meant something to me. I could lose my money, my mind, my status, my following, and my successes, but I cannot lose YOU.

I LOVE YOU!

One in the SAME. We are both 2yrs Old.

MY FAVORITE PICTURE OF US!

~CHAPTER NINE~

My Prayers Are For You

Every chance I get, I pray for you. I pray for your health and well-being. I pray for your safety and future prosperity. I pray that you will be a good human being who is kind-hearted and respectful and will show empathy to others. I pray that you will be successful in your own right. I pray that you will always make responsible decisions. But, mostly, I pray that this hard, cruel world will never make you a victim of its hatred and racism. I pray that all of your life lessons will come with very few bumps and bruises.

Now, it makes sense to me when my mom, your G-ma, would worry about me and your Uncle Tim. I see now, as a parent, that your Mother and I will never be comfortable with completely trusting others with your safety. WE WILL ALWAYS WORRY about you, Son. So just know that, not only do I pray for you, but Mommy prays for you. Nana and G-ma pray for you, and all of your family prays for you too.

When I look at you now I see so much potential for your life and I know it's God who has blessed you with all that you have inside of you. You are extremely intelligent and you have an infectious smile. I'm telling you now, that smile is going to make you a lot of money someday.

As your father I will protect you, but I will also be there to teach you the hard lessons of life that you need to learn. I won't try to keep you from all of the harsh realities as that wouldn't be fair to you; there will be growing pains and hard lessons learned. I want you to have an edge about you. I want you to know and understand pain and sacrifice as well as injustice. I want you to have a voice to speak up when things aren't right or when they just don't make sense.

    I pray that, when you open your mouth, you will know what to say and when to say it. I pray that you will be calculating, always having responsibility in the forefront of your mind and understanding that being a servant leader will get you a long way in life. I pray that you understand what having empathy for your fellow man and woman means and that you remain conscious of the fact that your life can change at any time. So, don't ever look down on someone else's misfortune because it could easily be you in those same shoes.

You will run into manipulators and those who will try to test your kindness. I hope you always see the wolf in sheep's clothing, Son. Again, some of this your little six-year-old mind won't get right now but trust me, as you get older, this will all be valuable information. Being your father will be more than just buying you gifts. It will be taking time to teach you and guide you all the days of my life.

I tell you, when God gave us to each other, He made a match that could have only come from heaven. I have so many plans for you. I have so many things I want to put into your mental toolbox for you to share with your own children someday.

I look forward to countless conversations that you and I will have.

I pray that when you read this book and fully understand what everything means, that you will see how much I care about you. I pray you see that, no matter what I do in life, I will always honor you because you mean that much to me. I pray that you will always know that, no matter what, I WAS NEVER ASHAMED to tell you that I LOVE and CARE FOR YOU, and that I'M VERY PROUD OF YOU. You will never have to look elsewhere for a father figure because I'M RIGHT HERE.

I LOVE YOU!

~CHAPTER TEN~

Love and Protect Your Mommy

Listen to me very closely. No matter what you do in life, no matter how big you get, no matter how successful you may become, always remember these words I'm about to say to you; **LOVE AND PROTECT YOUR MOTHER ALWAYS.**

This is the woman who carried you for nine months. This is the woman who will sacrifice for you and give you her last. This is the woman who will LOVE you even when you are dead wrong and still call you her baby. This is the woman who will hug and hold you when your first heartbreak happens and the woman who will turn into a bear if she sees anyone trying to hurt you. YOU must PROTECT , RESPECT, HONOR, OBEY, LISTEN, TAKE CARE OF, and LOVE YOUR MOTHER with all that you have because YOU WILL NEVER HAVE ANOTHER ONE!

I want you to see the strength in your mother, as well as the fragile nature of her womanhood. Take that same understanding and use it when you begin having your own relationships.

When I was a young boy, one thing I never wanted to do was disappoint my mother. I never wanted to see her cry and I always did what I was supposed to do so that she would not have to sacrifice as much. My heart was soft for my mother and, to this day, it still is. If she calls me for anything and I have it, I give it to her without hesitation.

That's what I want you to do. I want you to help make your mommy's life easier. I don't want you to give her problems or anything to worry about. DO NOT MAKE HER WORRY ABOUT YOU. Do not lie to her, ever. Don't break her heart. Don't ever go against her in malicious ways because that's not right.

I see now how much you love your mommy. How you make her smile and how you light up her day. I see when you hold her and call her your "sweetie." I see how many kisses you try to give her. It's so funny because you are so dramatic with it, but I know deep down inside that she loves your sweet playfulness and hopes you'll always do this, even when you get older. These moments will last a lifetime in her mind, so make many moments like that for her, OK?

I also want you to know that I will always respect and care for mommy despite all of us not being in the same household. We are good friends and we have one purpose in life and that is to raise you together as a team. There will always be love between us because of you. I think that is very important for children to know when their parents aren't together anymore. YOU ARE NOT THE BLAME FOR ANYTHING. Don't you ever think that.

There is no competition between your parents. If she gives you direction, I will not go against her and she will not go against me. We are, and will continue to be, a parenting team, buddy.

Well, my prince, this special book is about to come to an end. I hope that when you are fully able to understand all that I've written in it, you'll know how special it is to me to give this to you and share it with the world. I live to show my LOVE for you. Until another book is written to you and about you, I will end this one by saying, as I have, at the end of every chapter………..

I LOVE YOU!

ALWAYS TODAY. ALWAYS TOMORROW. ALWAYS FOREVER!

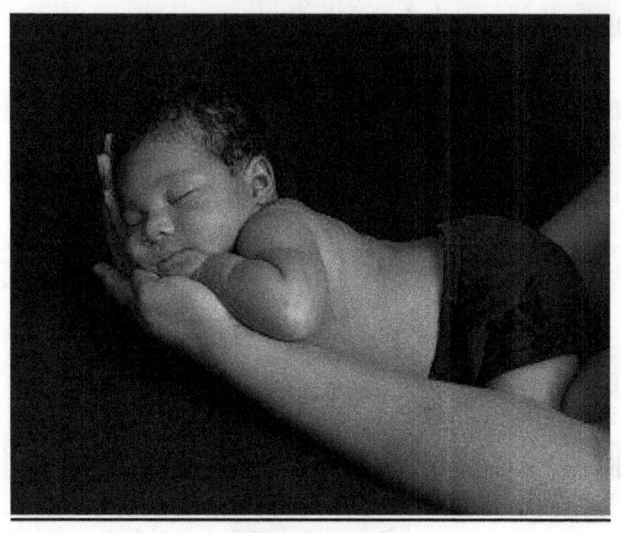

The Jordan Song

Jordan Is My...Jordan Is My...Baby Boy...Baby Boy

I Love My Baby Jordan...I Miss My Baby Jordan...Yes I Do...Yes I Do.

I Am the King...You Are the Prince....Mommy is The Queen...Mommy is the Queen

We Love You Little Jordan Poo... Yes We Really Really Do... We Love You...Jordan Pooooooooooo!

IT WILL NEVER BE THE END…….

ONLY NEW BEGINNINGS!!!!!!!

The Lion and His Cub

#UNBREAKABLE

Epilogue

This will always be a special book to me because I'm gifting it to my son as his first piece of TRUTHFUL literature that he will always be able to refer too. I knew when he was born that I would devote my life to him and create special moments so that he would always know that he meant the world to me. I hope and pray that this book will open up the minds and hearts not only to fathers to their sons but parents to their children. We have a dangerous climate in our world today and we as parents have to be more conscious of what our children need as it pertains to guidance and answers. Hopefully this will be a great start.

www.ingramcontent.com/pod-product-compliance
Lightning Source LLC
Chambersburg PA
CBHW070101100426
42743CB00012B/2626